D0938663

EXTREME MACHINES

TRUCKS

IAN GRAHAM

A+

Smart Apple Media

This book has been published in cooperation with Franklin Watts.

Created for Franklin Watts by Q2A Creative
Editor: Chester Fisher,
Designer: Sudakshina Basu,
Picture Researcher: Jyoti Sethi,

PICTURE CREDITS
Front cover: Western Star Trucks Back cover: STRANA
pp. 1 main (Kenworth), 4 bottom (National Motor Museum, Beaulieu), 5 top (Alan Nash www.steam-up.co.uk), 5 bottom (National Motor Museum, Beaulieu), 6 bottom (The Sparwood and District Chamber of Commerce), 7 top (Liebherr Holding GmbH), 8 bottom (Photos courtesy of Mack Trucks, Inc. All rights reserved.), 9 top (The Mack Trucks Historical Museum), 9 middle (Kenworth), 10 middle (Terex-Demag GmbH & Co.KG),11 bottom (Liebherr Holding GmbH), 12-13 bottom (Oshkosh Truck Corporation),13 top (U.S. Army Photo By: Kimberly Lee), 13 bottom (BIGFOOT 4X4, Inc.),14 bottom (Kenworth), 15 middle (NASA), 15 right (NASA) 16 top (Peterbilt), 17 middle (Kenworth), 18 top (Western Star Trucks), 19 middle (Tim Ahlborn) 20 bottom (Adam Alberti), 21 top (Oshkosh Truck Corporation), 22 top (Nate Mecha), 23 top (STRANA), 23 bottom (STRANA), 24 top (BIGFOOT 4X4, Inc.), 25 bottom (BIGFOOT 4X4, Inc.), 26 bottom (National Motor Museum, Beaulieu), 27 top (DaimlerChrysler), 28 middle left (National Motor Museum, Beaulieu), 28 top right (National Motor Museum, Beaulieu), 29 middle left (National Motor Museum, Beaulieu), 29 middle right (National Motor Museum, Beaulieu), 29 bottom (National Motor Museum, Beaulieu).

Published in the United States by Smart Apple Media
2140 Howard Drive West, North Mankato, Minnesota 56003

Library of Congress Cataloging-in-Publication Data

Graham, Ian, 1953–
Trucks / by Ian Graham.
p. cm. — (Extreme machines)
Includes index.
ISBN-13: 978-1-59920-043-9
1. Trucks—Juvenile literature. I. Title.

TL230.15G73152 2007
629.224—dc22   2006030846

9 8 7 6 5 4 3 2 1

CONTENTS

CURIOUS CARRIERS

Trucks are vehicles that travel on roads to move goods wherever they need to go. Nearly everything you see around you was transported or delivered by a truck.

OUT IN THE COLD

Early trucks, such as the 1903 Vabis, were very different from trucks today. They were like farm carts, but they had an engine and steering wheel at the front. Drivers sat in the open, so if it rained, they were soaking wet! In cold weather, they wore heavy coats to stay warm.

RATTLE AND ROLL

Trucks such as the 1903 Vabis shook and rattled along the road because they had poor springs and thin solid tires. By the 1920s, tires filled with air, called pneumatic tires, made trucks more comfortable.

Early trucks, like this 1903 Vabis, had wooden wheels.

1903 VABIS

ENGINE	2-cylinder gasoline
POWER	9 horsepower (hp)
LOAD CARRIED	1.7 tons (1.5 t)
TOP SPEED	7.5 miles (12 km) per hour

STEAMING ALONG

Today, many trucks are powered by diesel engines, but the first trucks were steam-powered. A steam engine used fire to heat a tank of water. The expanding steam made the engine run. Steam trucks were still being made in the 1920s. The Foden C-type was a popular British steam truck at that time; it was one of the last steam trucks.

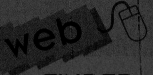

FINDER

http://www.scania.com/about/scaniahistory/
Visit this site for the history of Scania and Vabis trucks.
http://www.worldofsteam.com
See lots of information about steam trucks and other steam-powered vehicles at this site.

1920s FODEN C-TYPE "STEAMER"

ENGINE	Steam engine
POWER	23 hp
LOAD	6.7 tons (6 t)
TOP SPEED	16 miles (26 km) per hour

The Foden C-type looked like a steam locomotive on the road.

MEGA TRUCKS

The world's biggest trucks are the giant earth haulers that work in mines. Some of them are as big as a house! They carry dirt out of enormous holes in the ground where coal and other materials are mined.

TITAN

The biggest truck ever built was called the Terex Titan. Even when it was empty, it weighed as much as 175 cars. The Titan was built in 1978 and worked until 1990. Today it can be seen on display in the Canadian town of Sparwood, British Columbia.

LOCO POWER

The Terex Titan was powered by a railway locomotive engine, but the engine didn't drive the wheels! It was connected to a huge generator big enough to supply 250 homes with electricity. The generator ran four electric motors that drove the rear wheels.

Each of the Terex Titan's massive tires weighs as much as three cars!

The T282 B is so big that the driver is only half the height of its giant wheels.

131

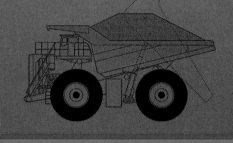

LIEBHERR T282 B

ENGINE	90-liter diesel
POWER	3,650 hp
EMPTY WEIGHT	252 tons (229 t)
LOADED WEIGHT	653 tons (592 t)

HEAVY HAULER

The Liebherr T282 B is the biggest earth-hauling truck in service today. It is smaller than the Terex Titan, but it can carry more. Fully loaded, it holds up to 800,000 pounds (363 t) of dirt. The driver's cab is so high that the driver has to climb a long stairway to reach it. Each of these giant trucks costs about $3 million.

TEREX TITAN

ENGINE	16-cylinder diesel
POWER	3,300 hp
EMPTY WEIGHT	259 tons (235 t)
LOADED WEIGHT	605 tons (549 t)

web

FINDER

http://www.sparwood.bc.ca/titaninf.htm
Information about the Terex Titan and a webcam to see the machine at work.
http://www.liebherr.com/me/en/40787.asp
Details of the Liebherr T282 truck.

MATERIAL MOVERS

Buildings, bridges, and roads are made from vast amounts of materials like concrete, bricks, steel, sand, and gravel. Trucks transport these materials to construction sites.

CONCRETE MIXER TRUCKS

Most trucks can carry different cargoes, but some trucks are specially designed to carry one type of cargo. The concrete mixer truck is one of these special-purpose trucks. The Mack FDM700 is unusual. Most mixer trucks pour concrete out at the back. The FDM700 pours it out at the front.

DRUM AND BLADES

The drum is loaded with sand, gravel, cement, and water. Then it spins to mix them up and make concrete. The drum must keep moving so that the concrete does not harden. It has blades or paddles inside to keep everything churning around. To unload, the drum turns in the opposite direction. The blades push the concrete out of the drum and down a chute.

MACK FDM700
CONCRETE MIXER TRUCK

ENGINE	12-liter diesel
POWER	320 hp
WEIGHT	28-40 tons (25-36 t)

DUMP TRUCKS

Loose materials like sand and gravel are carried
by road in dump trucks like the Kenworth T800.
When the truck finishes its journey, the driver
tips up the back of the truck. The back swings
open and all the sand or gravel spills onto
the ground.

One version
of the truck,
Kenworth T800,
is a tipper truck.

KENWORTH T800
DUMP TRUCK

Engine	10.3- to 12-liter diesel
Power	240 to 550 hp
Weight	30-65 tons (27-59 t)

web

FINDER

*http://www.macktrucks.com/default.aspx?
pageid=210*
The history of Mack trucks.
*http://www.kenworth.com/brochures/
WorkTrucks.pdf*
Kenworth trucks, including the T800 tipper truck.

GIANT LIFTERS

When something heavy has to be lifted into place, a truck crane is sometimes brought in for the job. A truck crane is a truck with a crane on top.

ONE TRUCK, TWO CABS

The Terex-Demag AC-200 is a modern truck crane. It has two cabs. The cab at the front is for driving the truck. Another cab farther back is for operating the crane. The crane boom is made in seven pieces that slide inside each other to make it small enough to travel on roads with other traffic.

Boom

Up to 8 of the AC-200's 10 wheels can turn to steer around tight bends.

Cab

Cab

TEREX-DEMAG AC-200 TRUCK CRANE

TRUCK ENGINE	516 hp
CRANE ENGINE	231 hp
LENGTH OF BOOM	222 feet (67.8 m)
MAXIMUM LIFT	221 tons (200 t)

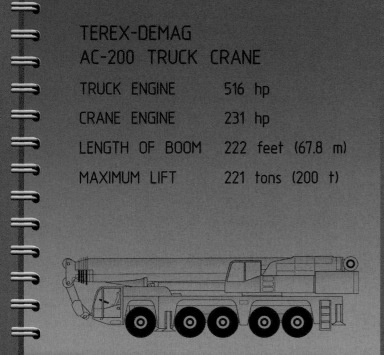

STAYING UPRIGHT

Before a truck crane like the AC-200 lifts anything, it puts out legs on each side. They are called outriggers, and they stop the crane from toppling over. Powerful "pushers" called hydraulic rams push the boom up. The parts of the boom slide out until the boom is the right length.

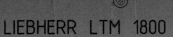

LIEBHERR LTM 1800

TRUCK ENGINE	598 hp diesel	LENGTH OF BOOM	197 feet (60 m)
CRANE ENGINE	408 hp diesel	MAXIMUM LIFT	882 tons (800 t)

KEEPING YOUR BALANCE

The Liebherr LTM 1800 is a truck crane that can lift loads four times heavier than the 220-ton (200-t) crane. A heavy counterweight is fixed at the rear of the crane to enable it to lift heavy loads safely. It balances the weight of the load. To lift heavier loads, a heavier counterweight is used.

FINDER

http://www.demag24.com/r_en/
Terex-Demag truck crane details.
http://www.liebherr.com/at/en/
Information and pictures of the Liebherr truck cranes.

The LTM 1800 has 16 wheels to spread its weight.

MILITARY MOVERS

Armies need to move very heavy equipment, including tanks. The trucks they use are some of the biggest, heaviest, and longest vehicles allowed on public roads.

TRANSPORTING TANKS

The biggest army truck is the Oshkosh M1070 Heavy Equipment Transporter (HET). It pulls the King GTS100 Heavy Equipment Trailer. Together, they can move a 79-ton (72 t) battle tank.

SPREADING THE WEIGHT

The HET and its trailer are so heavy that they could sink into soft ground. To prevent them from getting stuck, the trailer has a total of 40 wheels to spread the vehicle's great weight over the ground. When the driver turns the tractor's wheels, the trailer's front and back wheels turn too, to help steer this massive vehicle around curves.

The Oshkosh HET hauls the U.S. Army's M1 Abrams tanks.

The Overland Train's control rig carried a crew of six.

OVERLAND TRAIN

In the 1950s, the U.S. Army needed a big transporter to carry supplies to remote outposts in any climate.
One vehicle they tried was the Overland Train. It is still the longest land vehicle ever built. It had a truck called the control rig in front of 12 cargo cars. Each car had four wheels and each wheel was powered by its own electric motor.

LETOURNEAU OVERLAND TRAIN

ENGINE	600-hp diesel
WEIGHT	440 tons (400 t)
LENGTH	572 feet (174 m)
CREW	6
TOP SPEED	20 miles (32 km) per hour

OSHKOSH M1070 HEAVY EQUIPMENT TRANSPORTER AND KING GTS100 HEAVY EQUIPMENT TRAILER

ENGINE	18-liter
POWER	700 hp
UNLOADED WEIGHT	49.5 tons (45 t)
LOADED WEIGHT	130 tons (118 t)

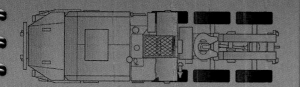

FINDER

http://www.oshkoshtruck.com/defense/ products~het~1070f.cfm
Find out more about the newest Oshkosh Heavy Equipment Transporter.
http://www.army.mil/fact_files_site/het
Information about the Oshkosh Heavy Equipment Transporter from the U.S. Army.

HEAVY HAULERS

The biggest and heaviest loads need special vehicles to move them. Some are carried on supersized trailers pulled by ordinary trucks, but the most extreme loads need specially designed vehicles.

A Kenworth T800 transports a telescope mirror packed safely inside a steel case.

OVERSIZE LOAD

MOUNTAIN CLIMBING

In 2003, when a giant mirror had to be delivered to a telescope on top of a mountain, a special vehicle was needed. The mirror was more than 27 feet (8 m) across. It had to be carried up a steep, narrow and winding road to the Mount Graham International Observatory in Arizona.

BOXING CLEVER

A Kenworth T800 truck was paired with a special trailer for the job. The mirror was carried inside a steel box to protect it. The mirror and the box weighed 55 tons (50 t). The box was held up on end so that it would fit between the trees at the sides of the narrow road.

KENWORTH T800 HEAVY HAULER

ENGINE	565-hp diesel
WEIGHT CARRIED	90 tons (82 t)
SPEED ON MOUNTAIN ROAD	4 miles (6 km) per hour

SUPER MOVERS

The most extreme transporters are the crawler-transporters that take space shuttles to the launchpad. Each transporter is 131 feet (40 m) long and weighs more than 70 normal trucks. Huge diesel engines drive electric generators that power electric motors. The motors drive eight giant trucks at a slow walking speed.

A crawler-transporter moves the space shuttle Discovery and its launch platform to the launchpad.

NASA CRAWLER-TRANSPORTER

MOTORS	16 electric drive motors
ENGINES	Two 2,750-hp diesel engines
WEIGHT	3,000 tons (2,721 t)
TOP SPEED	2 miles (3 km) per hour

FINDER

http://science.ksc.nasa.gov/
facilities/crawler.html
Details of NASA's giant
crawler-transporters.

LONG HAUL

Road trains are common in Australia.

The biggest trucks on the road haul goods and materials across the longest distances. They can not be much wider than other trucks because they must fit on ordinary roads, but they are much longer.

TRAINS ON THE ROAD

The trucks that transport goods and materials across Australia are so long that they are called road trains. The front part of a road train is a very powerful tractor. It has to be powerful because it is pulling a big, heavy load. In Australia, the tractor is called a prime mover. The prime mover pulls a semitrailer and at least two more trailers. The longest road trains can have six or more trailers.

FILLING UP WITH FUEL

There are not many fuel stations on the long roads that cross Australia. Road trains need to carry a lot more fuel than other trucks. They have enough fuel to drive for about 1,000 miles (1,600 km).

CENTIPEDE TRUCKS

Most American trucks are not allowed to weigh more than 40 tons (36 t), but some states allow heavier trucks. Michigan is famous for its heavyweight trucks. The longest of these trucks have two trailers with lots of wheels. They are known as Michigan Doubles, Michigan Specials, or Michigan Centipedes. They can weigh up to 82 tons (74 t).

AUSTRALIAN ROAD TRAIN

ENGINE	650-hp diesel
TRAILERS	3
LENGTH	174 feet (53 m)
LOADED WEIGHT	154 tons (140 t)

Michigan trucks are some of the biggest and heaviest on U.S. roads.

MICHIGAN CENTIPEDE

ENGINE	400- to 500-hp diesel
TRAILERS	2
LENGTH	100 feet (30 m)
LOADED WEIGHT	82 tons (74 t)

web FINDER

http://www.westernstar.com.au
Find out more about Australian road trains.
http://www.ebroadcast.com.au/ecars/Places/Au/Road-Trains.html
Details of Australian road trains.

EMERGENCY!

One of the most important special-purpose trucks is the fire engine. It is designed to carry a team of firefighters and their equipment to a fire as quickly as possible.

WHICH TRUCK'S WHICH?

There are different types of fire engines. Pumper trucks, or pumps, send water through hoses. Tanker trucks carry extra water. Rescue trucks carry equipment to rescue people trapped in vehicles. Ladder trucks carry ladders that firefighters can use to fight a fire from high above the ground. The Seagrave Force 100 is a ladder truck.

TURNTABLE LADDER

The Force 100's ladder extends to a height of 100 feet (30 m). The ladder stands on a turntable so that it can be turned in any direction. A water hose is attached to the end of the ladder. Compartments in the truck hold all the equipment the firefighters need, including at least 1,000 feet (305 m) of hose.

A Seagrave ladder truck from the Fire Department of New York.

An Oshkosh Striker airport fire truck from Washington

AIRPORT RESCUE

The Oshkosh Striker 4500 is a fire engine specially designed for airports. It can fight a fire with water or foam. Foam is sprayed over spilled fuel to keep it from catching fire. The water or foam is pumped from nozzles, called turrets, on the truck's roof and front bumper.

OSHKOSH STRIKER 4500 FIRE TRUCK

ENGINE	950-hp diesel
TOP SPEED	70 miles (112 km) per hour
WATER TANK	4,500 gallons (17,033 l)
FOAM TANK	630 gallons (2,385 l)

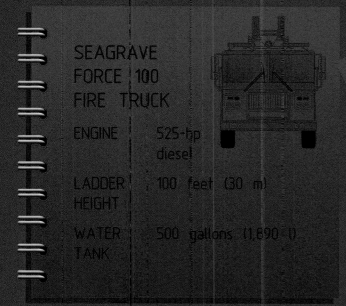

SEAGRAVE FORCE 100 FIRE TRUCK

ENGINE	525-hp diesel
LADDER HEIGHT	100 feet (30 m)
WATER TANK	500 gallons (1,890 l)

web

FINDER

http://www.seagrave.com/Products/Aerials/Force/Force.html
Details of Seagrave Force fire engines.
http://www.oshkoshtruck.com/airportmunicipal/home.cfm
Meet the Striker airport fire engine.

SPORT TRUCKS

A racing pick-up truck hugs the ground as it rounds a turn.

Trucks make surprisingly good racing vehicles. Small pickup trucks and even big rig tractors take part in truck races.

PICKUP RACING

Pickup trucks, or utility trucks, are small, open-back trucks about the same size as a car. Pickups used for racing look like ordinary trucks on the road, but they are specially built for racing. They are lighter, more powerful, and faster than ordinary trucks. They are also designed to be safer at racing speeds. The driver is protected by a strong metal frame that goes all around the driver's cab.

NASCAR CRAFTSMAN RACING PICKUP TRUCK

ENGINE	5.8-liter
POWER	700 hp
WEIGHT	3,400 pounds (1,540 kg)
TOP SPEED	190 miles (300 km) per hour

CHANGING SHAPE

The open back of an ordinary pickup truck "catches" a lot of air and slows the truck down. This doesn't matter for a truck on the road, but it would slow down a racing truck too much. The back of a racing pickup is covered to give it a smoother shape. This helps it move through the air faster.

SUPER TRUCKS

Super Trucks are big rig tractors with super powerful engines. Like racing pickups, Super Trucks are specially built for the race track. Compared to the ordinary trucks on the roads, these racing machines are stronger, more streamlined, and more than twice as powerful.

SUPER TRUCK RACING TRUCK

ENGINE	11.1-liter diesel
POWER	1,000 hp
WEIGHT	12,800 pounds (5,800 kg)
TOP SPEED	100 miles (160 km) per hour

Super Truck racing engines are twice as powerful as standard truck engines.

web FINDER

http://www.worldofmotorsport.com/pickups.php
Find out more about pick-up truck racing.
http://www.tricklefan.com/manual/div_truck.html
Read about NASCAR Craftsman Truck racing in the U.S.
http://trucktrend.com/roadtests/ultimate/163_0402_trkracing
Pictures and information about Super Truck racing.

MONSTERS

Monster trucks are specially built trucks with very big wheels. They entertain crowds of spectators at special events by racing, jumping in the air, and crushing other vehicles by driving over them.

Changing a tire on Bigfoot 5 is a big job!

BIGFOOT 5 MONSTER TRUCK

ENGINE	7.5-liter
HEIGHT	15 feet 6 inches (4.7 m)
WEIGHT (with 4 tires)	28,000 pounds (12,700 kg)
WEIGHT (with 8 tires)	38,000 pounds (17,240 kg)

THE BIGGEST MONSTER

The biggest monster truck is called Bigfoot 5. The truck's body is dwarfed by its giant wheels. The tires were made for the U.S. Army's Overland Train (see page 13). Each tire stands 10 feet (3 m) high and weighs as much as a small car!

DOUBLE TROUBLE

When Bigfoot 5 made its first appearance in 1986, it had eight wheels—four giant wheels at the front and four at the back. It instantly became the world's tallest, widest, and heaviest monster truck. It still holds the record today.

WE HAVE LIFTOFF!

Monster trucks are famous for their amazing stunts, including jumping over other vehicles. In 1999, Bigfoot 14 jumped over a Boeing 727 airliner. It set two records. As it headed toward the jump, it reached a world record speed for a monster truck—69.3 miles (111.5 km) per hour. It also set the record for the longest-ever monster truck jump—a distance of 202 feet (61.5 m).

web

FINDER
http://www.bigfoot4x4.com/bf5.html
Read about Bigfoot 5.
http://www.bigfoot4x4.com/bf14.html
Bigfoot 14's page.

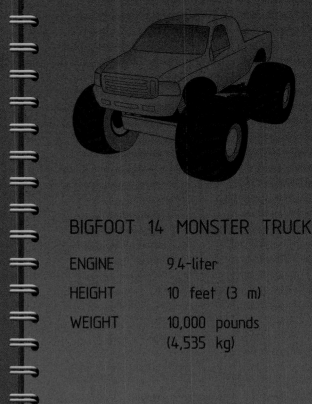

BIGFOOT 14 MONSTER TRUCK

ENGINE	9.4-liter
HEIGHT	10 feet (3 m)
WEIGHT	10,000 pounds (4,535 kg)

Bigfoot 14 has wowed the crowds with its amazing jumps since 1994.

FUTURE FREIGHTERS

Truck companies are always thinking about what future trucks might be like. They try out new ideas by making vehicles called "concept" trucks. Ideas that work well are then built into trucks in the future.

CURVY CAB

The Renault Radiance concept truck shows that trucks don't have to look dull. Most trucks are square and box-shaped, but the Radiance has a more curvy, streamlined body. The driver's cab has big windows to give a good view. Cameras built into the truck's body show spots that are hard for the driver to see.

SMART INSIDE

The inside of the driver's cab is very futuristic. The driver uses a smart card instead of a key to get into the cab and start the engine. The cab looks like a modern office.

RENAULT RADIANCE

BODY	Streamlined shape
FEATURES	Smart-card entry
	Foldaway gear lever
	Mirrors replaced by cameras
	Windows can be darkened

The streamlined shape of the Radiance means it burns less fuel.

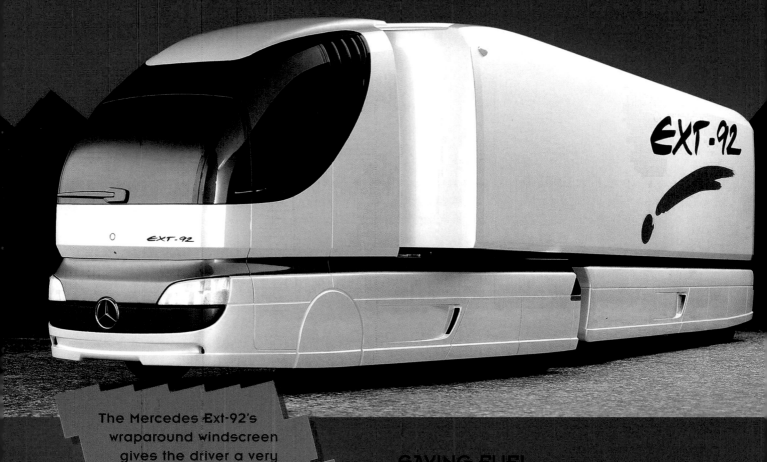

The Mercedes Ext-92's wraparound windscreen gives the driver a very clear view.

MERCEDES EXT-92

BODY   Fully streamlined
            shape

FEATURES   Smart-card entry

            Mirrors replaced
            by cameras

            Radar warns of
            vehicles too close

            Driver's seat in
            the center

            Windows can be
            darkened

SAVING FUEL

The Mercedes Ext-92 (European Experimental Truck) was designed in 1992, but it still looks very futuristic today. Its amazing shape is designed to let it move through air very easily. Just changing a truck's shape can save fuel, making the truck less expensive to run.

FINDER

http://www.cardesignnews.com/news/2004/ 041220renault-radiance
See more pictures of the Renault Radiance.
http://www.germancarfans.com/news.cfm/newsid/ 2041231.002/page/2/mercedes/1.html
Read about the Mercedes Ext-92 concept truck.

TIMELINE

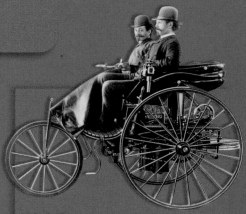

1769

French military engineer Nicolas Cugnot builds a steam-powered tractor. It is the first vehicle to move under its own power. A second tractor built by Cugnot in 1770 still exists today.

1861

German engineer Nikolaus Otto builds a new type of gasoline engine. It is the first practical alternative to the steam engine.

1885

German engineer Karl Benz builds the world's first practical automobile powered by a gasoline engine. It is a three-wheeler with a top speed of about 8 miles (13 km) per hour.

1801

British engineer Richard Trevithick builds a steam-powered carriage.

1829

The first steam-powered fire engines are invented by John Braithwaite and John Ericsson in London, England. At first they are unpopular because they take work away from people who operate hand-powered water pumps. Other people think they are not powerful enough.

1862

Belgian inventor Étienne Lenoir builds the first successful internal combustion engine and also the first vehicle powered by an internal combustion engine.

1887

German engineers Gottlieb Daimler and Wilhelm Maybach produce the first four-wheel automobile powered by an internal combustion engine. It had been built originally as a horse-drawn carriage.

1862

Three steam-powered fire engines go on display at the International Exhibition held in Hyde Park, London.

1888

Scotsman John Boyd Dunlop invents the pneumatic (air-filled) rubber tire. It was used on bicycles first, but pneumatic tires were later fitted to larger vehicles, including trucks.

1858

The first successful steam-powered fire engine starts work. Soon, the "steamers" can pump water faster than hand-operated fire pumps.

1863

Ten steam-powered fire engines, seven British and three American, take part in a three-day trial at Crystal Palace, London. An engine built by the British Merryweather company wins.

1889

Daimler and Maybach build the first automobile that is designed from the start as an automobile.

1892

French engineer Rudolf Diesel invents a new type of engine called a diesel engine that will later power most trucks.

1896

The 1.6-ton (1.5 t) Daimler Phoenix becomes the world's first gasoline-powered truck.

1897

Rudolf Diesel builds the first practical diesel engine. The 25-hp engine is simple and works well. It soon becomes very popular, making Diesel very wealthy.

1903

The first gasoline-powered fire engines start work in London.

1913

Trucks are fitted with wheels that can be replaced. Trucks start carrying spare wheels.

1914

The first tow truck is built in the U.S.

1914

American August Fruehauf builds the first semi from a tractor unit pulling a separate semitrailer.

1925

Pneumatic, or air-filled, truck tires begin to replace solid rubber tires.

1930

The first diesel-powered trucks are built. They begin to replace trucks powered by steam or gasoline.

1950

Most large trucks—such as the one below—are now powered by diesel engines.

1951

Power steering makes it easier to turn the steering wheels of heavy vehicles such as trucks.

1954

Standard sizes of freight containers are introduced.

1983

The heaviest trucks allowed on British roads are set at 42 tons (38 t).

1992

Mercedes unveils its futuristic Ext-92 concept truck.

2004

Renault shows its Radiance concept truck in Hanover, Germany.

GLOSSARY

BOOM

A crane's arm, also called a jib.

BIG RIG

A truck with a tractor pulling a semitrailer.

CENTIPEDE

A very long and heavy truck with lots of wheels. Centipedes are common in Michigan.

CONCEPT TRUCK

A truck built to show how future trucks might look. "Concept" means idea.

COUNTERWEIGHT

A heavy weight hung from one side of a truck crane to balance the load being lifted by the crane so that the truck does not fall over.

CU IN

Cubic inch—a small space measuring one inch long, one inch wide, and one inch high. The size of an engine is measured in cubic inches.

DIESEL ENGINE

A type of engine that powers most trucks. A diesel engine burns an oily fuel called diesel oil. Both of them are named after the man who invented the engine, Rudolf Diesel.

FIFTH WHEEL

The part of a big rig where the tractor (the front part) is joined to the semitrailer (the back part).

FREIGHT

Transported goods.

GENERATOR

A machine for making electricity.

HORSEPOWER (HP)

A unit of power. The power of an engine is measured in horsepower. A small family car might have an engine up to about 150 horsepower. Most trucks have engines of 300–600 horsepower.

INTERNAL COMBUSTION ENGINE

A type of engine. Its fuel (gasoline or diesel oil) is burned inside the engine instead of in a separate furnace. A modern truck engine is an internal combustion engine.

KPH

Kilometer per hour—a measurement of speed. A truck traveling at 40 kph takes one hour to go a distance of 40 kilometers. 40 kph is about the same speed as 25 miles per hour.

MONSTER TRUCK

A truck with huge wheels, built for racing, jumping, and crushing other vehicles to entertain crowds.

MPH

Miles per hour—a measurement of speed. A truck traveling at 25 mph takes one hour to go a distance of 25 miles. 25 mph is about the same speed as 40 kilometers per hour.

NASA

The National Aeronautics and Space Administration—the organization responsible for non-military space research and space flights in the U.S.

PICKUP TRUCK

A small type of truck with an open back for carrying goods and materials. Also called a utility truck.

ROAD TRAIN

A very long truck made from a tractor pulling a semitrailer and at least two more trailers. Road trains transport goods and materials in Australia.

SEMITRAILER

The back part of a big rig. The semitrailer is pulled by the tractor. It's called a semitrailer because it has no wheels at the front. The front rests on the back of the tractor.

STEAM ENGINE

An engine powered by steam. Fuel, such as wood or coal that is burned in a furnace, heats water in a tank. The water makes steam, and the steam makes the engine go.

STEAM TRUCK

A truck powered by a steam engine, also called a "steamer." Many trucks were steamers until the 1930s.

STREAMLINED

Shaped to move through air easily. A streamlined truck has a smooth, gently curving body.

TON

A unit of weight. A ton is the same as 2,000 pounds (907 kg).

TRACTOR

A vehicle that pulls a machine, trailer, or semitrailer. Farm tractors pull many kinds of machines for working on the land and dealing with crops. A truck tractor pulls a semitrailer.

Note to parents and teachers:
Every effort has been made to ensure that the Web sites in this book are suitable for children, that they are of the highest educational value, and that they contain no inappropriate or offensive material. However, because of the nature of the Internet, it is impossible to guarantee that the contents of these sites will not be altered. We strongly advise that Internet access be supervised by a responsible adult.

EXTREME MACHINES Trucks

INDEX